AAT Diploma in Accounting
Level 3
Business Awareness

TP03-8-0/323-0003

First edition 2021

ISBN 9781 5097 4024 6

e-ISBN 9781 5097 4395 7

British Library Cataloguing-in-Publication Data

A catalogue record for this book is available from the British Library

Published by
BPP Learning Media Ltd
BPP House, Aldine Place
142–144 Uxbridge Road
London W12 8AA

www.bpp.com/learningmedia

Printed in the United Kingdom

Your learning materials, published by BPP Learning Media Ltd, are printed on paper obtained from traceable sustainable sources.

Welcome to BPP Learning Media's ATT **Passcards** for **Business Awareness**.

- They **save you time**. Important topics are summarised for you.
- They incorporate **diagrams** to kick start your memory.
- They follow the overall **structure** of the BPP Course Book, but BPP Learning Media's AAT **Passcards** are not just a condensed book. Each card has been separately designed for clear presentation. Topics are self-contained and can be grasped visually.
- AAT **Passcards** are still **just the right size** for pockets and bags.
- AAT **Passcards focus on the assessment** you will be facing.
- AAT **Passcards focus on the essential points** that you need to know in the workplace, or when completing your assessment.

Run through the complete set of **Passcards** as often as you can during your final revision period. The day before the assessment, try to go through the **Passcards** again! You will then be well on your way to completing the assessment successfully.

Good luck!

Contents

The BPP **Question Bank** contains activities and assessments that provide invaluable practice in the skills you need to complete this unit successfully.

1: Types of business

Exam questions will likely focus on three aspects:

1 *Can you identify the features of a particular business type*

2 *Can you correctly identify the nature of a business from a description given*

3 *Can you identify the most suitable type of business form in a given scenario*

Organisational aims:
- Profit motive
- Charitable aims
- Non-profit eg government

Manufacturers
- Tangible goods

Services
- Intangible
- Inseparable
- Variable
- Perishable

Information needs
- Profit motive
  - Sales, costs, profit, cash
- Charitable aims
  - Donations, grants, costs, progress towards objectives
- Non-profit
  - Economy, efficiency, effectiveness

Sole traders/partnerships

- No separate legal person
- Contract in own name(s)
- Pay income taxes
- Unlimited personal liability

Partnership regulation

- Agreement should cover
  - Profit share
  - Dispute resolution
  - Conduct of partners' meetings
  - Leavers/joiners/retirements
- PA 1890
  - Equal profit share
  - All partners indemnified
  - All partners see books
  - All partners manage
  - Any partner can block new joiner

Goodwill

- Business value > net assets
- Leavers will receive share
- Joiners need to buy a share

Incorporation

- File online with Co's House
- Certificate of Incorporation
- Separate legal entity

Public limited company (plc)

- Need a trading certificate
- £50,000 of shares
- 2+ directors & Co Secretary
- Must hold AGM
- Can obtain a listing
- File 9 months from year end

Private limited company (Ltd)

- Liability of member limited by
  o Shares (common)
  o Guarantee (rare)
- One director
- One shareholder
- No minimum capital required
- Co Secretary optional
- No AGM – use written resolutions
- File 6 months from year end

Directors' duties

- Fiduciary
  - To account
  - Conflicts of interest
  - Disclose
  - No secret profits
- Statutory
  - Obey articles
  - Promote long-term success
  - Independent judgement
  - Reasonable skill, care and diligence
  - Conflicts of interest
  - Third party benefits
  - Declare interest in transactions

Shareholders

- Most powers delegated to board
- Shareholders power used in:
  - AGM
  - GM
- Power via voting rights
  - OR >50% of votes cast
  - SR ≥75% of votes cast
  - Written resolutions in Ltd Co only

LLPs

- Very similar to companies, but:
  - Income tax for partners
  - All partners manage
  - Partnership agreement allowed
- Limited partnerships – LPA 1907
  - Incorporate separate legal entity
  - 1+ unlimited liability partner
  - Limited partners:
    - Can't manage
    - Can't withdraw capital

Financing a business

- Debt – borrow money
  - Cheap to arrange
  - Interest payable
  - Loans/overdraft/debentures
- Equity – more shares
  - Dividends payable
  - Issue to external investors will dilute holding of current owners

2: Organisational structure and governance

Topic List

Structures

Governance

Risk management

Stakeholders and role of finance

Exam questions will likely focus on three aspects:

1   *Suitable organisational structures*

2   *Identify suitable risk responses/controls*

3   *Identify stakeholders and how to manage them*

4   *Explain how the finance function supports others*

Functional
- Group by work specialism

Divisional
- Multiple functional set-ups
- Location/products

Matrix
- Cross-functional teams
- Suited to project working

Scalar chain
- Links from top to bottom

Span of control
- Number of subordinates

Organisations can be:
- Tall and narrow OR Flat and wide

Tall

MD
Divisional directors
Department managers
Section managers
Supervisors
Charge hands
Workers

Flat

MD
Department managers
Supervisors
Workers

Governance

- How a business is controlled
  - Risk reduction
  - Improved performance
  - Better perception

Centralised control

- Faster decisions
- Holistic view
- More control and standardisation

Decentralised control

- Managers empowered and motivated
- Localised decision making

Layers of management

- Corporate/strategic – set strategy
- Managerial – strategy into actions
- Operational – deliver goods/services

2: Organisational structure and governance

Risk

- Quantifiable dispersion of outcomes
- Upside – positive
- Downside – negative

Uncertainty

- Dispersion that can't be quantified

Risk management

- **T**ransfer – insurance
- **A**void – stop risky activity
- **R**educe – implement controls
- **A**ccept – work with the risk

Types of risk

- Strategic – long-term, co-wide
  - Business
    - Product
    - Environment
    - Stakeholders
    - Investment
  - Non-business
    - Financial
    - Event
- Operational – day-to-day, localised
  - IT, ethics, cyber, health and safety

Stakeholders
- Person(s) who have a stake in the organisation
  - Primary – directly affected
  - Secondary – indirectly affected
  - Internal – managers, employees
  - Connected – finance providers
  - External – all others
- Mendelow's Matrix
  - Map Power and Interest
  - Low & Low – minimal effort
  - Low & High – keep informed
  - High & Low – keep satisfied
  - High & High – key players

Role of the finance function
- Support other functions:
  - Operations – contribution analysis
  - Sales – pricing/promotions
  - HR – 3 Es
  - IT – cost v benefit analysis
  - Distribution – efficiency/outsourcing

2: Organisational structure and governance

3: The external environment

Topic List
Macro environment
Demand
Supply
Price
Sustainability

Exam questions are likely to focus on:

1   The impact of the external environment on a
    business (demand, supply, price)

2   Sustainability: What it is, and the costs and benefits
    of it to a business

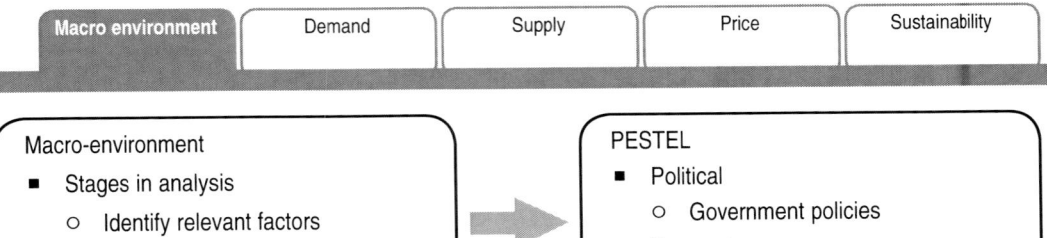

| Macro environment | Demand | Supply | Price | Sustainability |

Macro-environment

- Stages in analysis
  - Identify relevant factors
  - Consider their impact
  - Formulate responses

PESTEL

- Political
  - Government policies
- Economic
  - Interest rates/inflation
- Social
  - Demographics/trends
- Technical
  - Internet/Big data
- Environmental
  - Sustainability
- Legal
  - Trade regulations

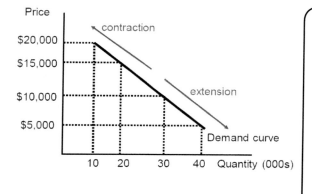

Demand

- As the price of a good falls then demand should rise

- Conditions of demand include

  - Normal v inferior v necessary goods

  - Price of substitutes

  - Price of complements

  - Tastes and preferences

  - Market expectations

- Changes to conditions can move the demand curve left or right

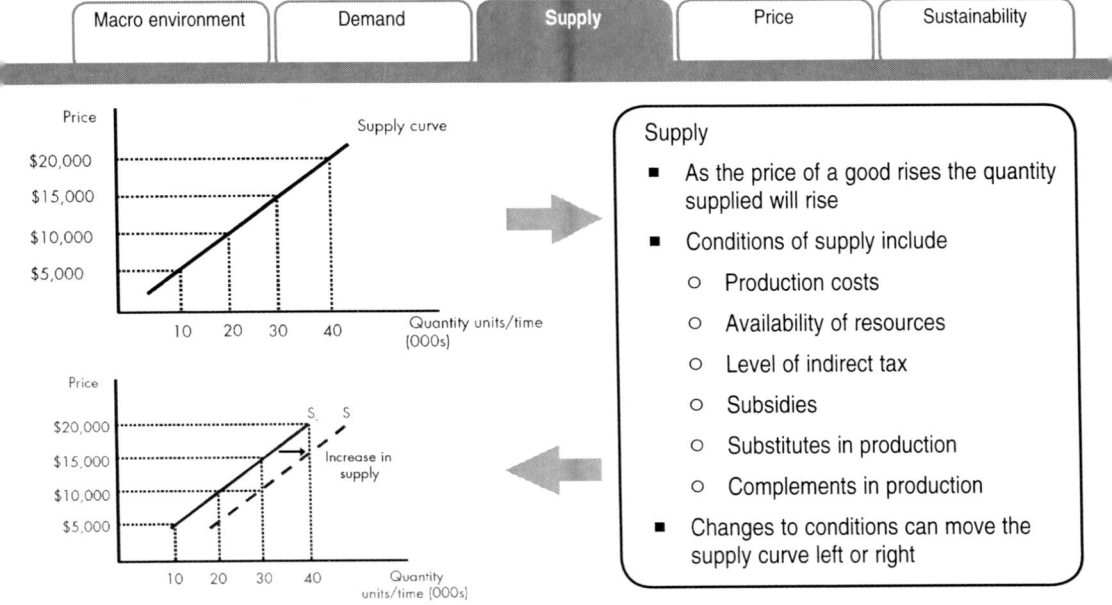

Supply

- As the price of a good rises the quantity supplied will rise
- Conditions of supply include
  - Production costs
  - Availability of resources
  - Level of indirect tax
  - Subsidies
  - Substitutes in production
  - Complements in production
- Changes to conditions can move the supply curve left or right

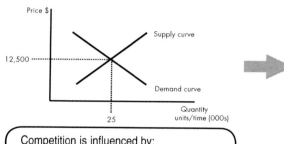

Competition is influenced by:
- Product features
- The number of buyers and sellers
- Barriers to entry
- Location
- Availability of information

Price
- Shortages
  - Demand > Supply
  - Prices will rise
- Surplus
  - Demand < Supply
  - Prices will fall
- Price mechanism
  - Signalling
  - Rationing and allocation
  - Rewarding

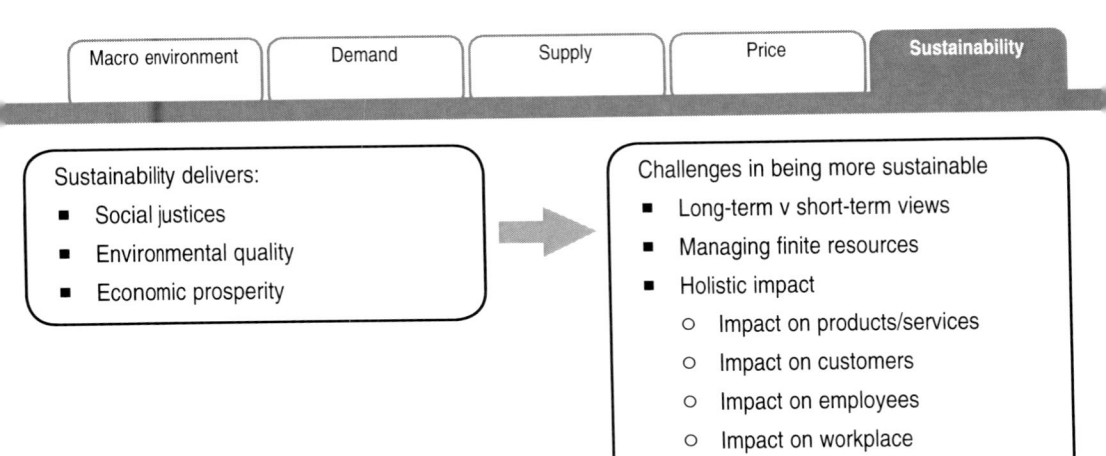

Sustainability delivers:

- Social justices
- Environmental quality
- Economic prosperity

Challenges in being more sustainable

- Long-term v short-term views
- Managing finite resources
- Holistic impact
  - Impact on products/services
  - Impact on customers
  - Impact on employees
  - Impact on workplace
  - Impact on supply chain
  - Impact on business functions and processes

4: Professional ethics for accountants

Topic List

Ethical codes

Fundamental principles

Threats and safeguards

Exam questions may focus on:

1   *Identifying relevant ethical principles – the five fundamental principles.*

2   *Explaining the actions that can be taken to combat ethical threats.*

3   *Explain the difference between principles and rules-based approaches to ethics.*

The AAT Code comprises:
- Five fundamental principles
- Conceptual framework
- Guidance and illustrations

Principles-based approach
- Flexible
- Illustrates principles
- No loopholes to exploit

BUT
- Can be subjective
- Inconsistent actions
- Guidelines can become rules

Rules-based approach
- Specific rules for scenarios
- Consistent application
- Easy to identify breaches

BUT
- Rules = possible loopholes
- Can't have a rule for everything
- Ethics not always black and white

Five fundamental principles

- **Objectivity** – ability to make judgements and decisions free from bias.

- **Professional competence and due care** – an accountant should only take on tasks that they are technically competent to perform. Also, a duty to stay technically up-to-date.

- **Professional behaviour** – not doing anything that will discredit the AAT.

- **Integrity** – acting in a manner that is honest and straightforward in all professional and business relationships.

- **Confidentiality** – a duty to safeguard any information in your possession unless there is a legal or professional duty to disclose. Exceptions are where:

  ○ Permitted by law

  ○ Permitted by client/employers

  ○ Required by law

  ○ Permitted by professional right or duty

Threats

- **Self-interest** – put yourself before your employer/client.

- **Self-review** – review your own work, threat to integrity and objectivity.

- **Advocacy** – promote a position or belief beyond the point of professional objectivity.

- **Familiarity** – close relationships compromise integrity and objectivity.

- **Intimidation** – physical, mental or financial.

Safeguards

- Educations

- Corporate governance

- Ethical codes

- Disciplinary action

- Complaints systems

- Corporate oversight

- Policies and procedures

- Recruitment controls

- Employee performance systems

- Communication channels eg whistleblowing

5: Ethical conflicts

Topic List

Consequences

Identify breaches

Resolving dilemmas

Disciplinary action

Money Laundering

Exam questions may focus on:

1   Identify ethical issues in a scenario.

2   Explain the implications for accountants that act unethically.

3   Describe best practice in dealing with ethical conflicts.

4   Describe the elements of money laundering, and how to react should suspicious activities take place.

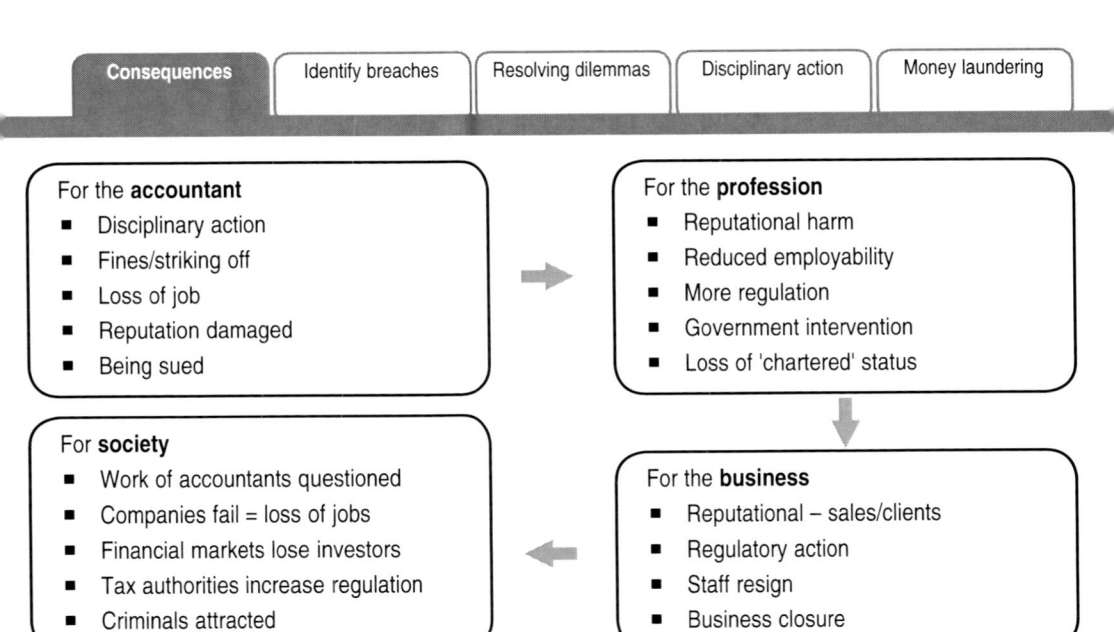

For the **accountant**
- Disciplinary action
- Fines/striking off
- Loss of job
- Reputation damaged
- Being sued

For the **profession**
- Reputational harm
- Reduced employability
- More regulation
- Government intervention
- Loss of 'chartered' status

For **society**
- Work of accountants questioned
- Companies fail = loss of jobs
- Financial markets lose investors
- Tax authorities increase regulation
- Criminals attracted

For the **business**
- Reputational – sales/clients
- Regulatory action
- Staff resign
- Business closure

Societal values	**Personal** values
■ National law	■ Internal beliefs
■ National customs	■ Religious beliefs
Organisational values	**Professional** values
■ Transparency	■ Professional bodies
■ Reporting on time and openly	■ Five fundamental principles
■ Paying fair process	
■ Fair treatment of staff	

Other issues

- ■ Pressure from colleagues/family
- ■ Offer of gifts – when is hospitality a bribe?
- ■ Personal circumstance – financial hardship

5: Ethical conflicts

Checklist

1. Check all the facts
2. Is the issue 'ethical'?
3. Identify fundamental principles
4. Refer to internal guidance
5. Consider courses of action
6. Seek professional advice
7. Disassociate from the situation

Be sure to:

- Be transparent
- Consider all affected stakeholders
- Act fairly

Reporting

8. Be confident that a breach has occurred
9. Follow internal processes eg report to MLRO
10. Seek confidential advice if you are still uncertain
11. Make an external disclosure if required. **Take legal advice before doing so.**

Action can be taken by:
- Employer
- AAT
  - 42 days' notice
  - 28 days to submit written statement
  - Hearing – balance of probabilities
  - Tribunal makes a decision
  - Misconduct = penalties
    - Expulsion or suspension
    - Reprimand
    - Fines
    - Membership withdrawn
- May also have broken the law
- Act fairly

Be sure to be:
- Transparent
- Consider all affected stakeholders
- Act fairly

Professional negligence
- Professional indemnity insurance
- Cover based on higher of gross fee income or set amount:
  - Sole trade 2.5x or £50k
  - Partnership 2.5x or £100k
  - Ltd Co 2.5x or £100k

Process of Money laundering

1. Placement – move proceeds of crime
2. Layering – move money around
3. Integration – withdrawn as apparently legitimate income

Offences of money laundering

4. Laundering – 14 years + Fine
5. Failure to report – 5 years + Fine
6. Tipping off – 2 years + Fine

Suspect Money Laundering?

- Report to your MLRO
- MLRO submits an SAR
- Do not report to anyone else
- Correctly submitted SAR = full immunity for the accountant

6: Technology and data

Exam questions may focus on:

1   Identify the different types of technology that an organisation can deploy.

2   Explain the advantages that different types of technology have.

3   Describe the data protection legal requirements, and the consequences for organisations that breach these.

4   Describe the cyber-attacks that organisations face, and the cyber-defences available to protect them.

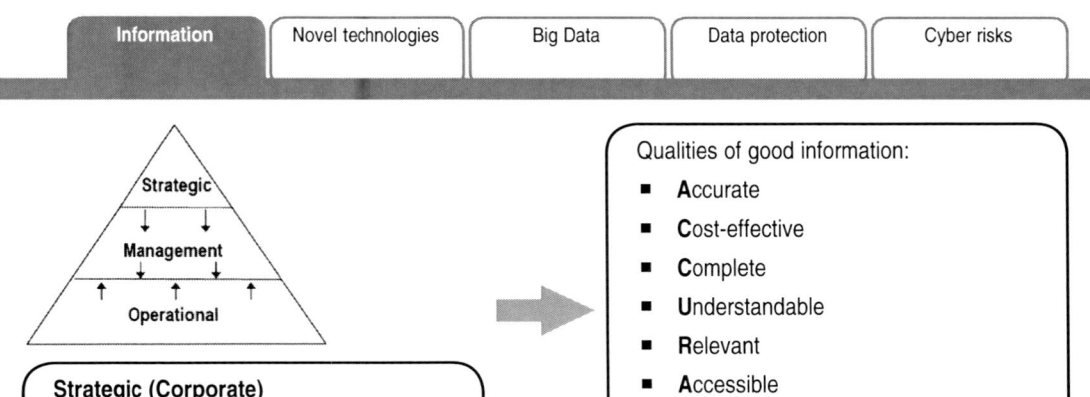

Strategic (Corporate)
- Unstructured, external, long-term

Management
- Semi-structured, internal, and external

Operational
- Structured, internal, short-term

Qualities of good information:
- **A**ccurate
- **C**ost-effective
- **C**omplete
- **U**nderstandable
- **R**elevant
- **A**ccessible
- **T**imely
- **E**asy to use

Emerging technologies in accountancy

- **Process automation** – data gathering, processing and analysis

- **Blockchain** – distributed ledgers, providing immutable records. This technology supports cryptocurrencies

- **AI** – using cognitive computing and machine learning to speed up processing and allow computers to search for patterns in data

- **Electronic signature** and **filing**

- **Cloud computing** and **cloud accounting** – allows access to systems from anywhere with internet connectivity

- **Outsourcing** – normally non-core activities

- **Offshoring** – outsource overseas to save cost

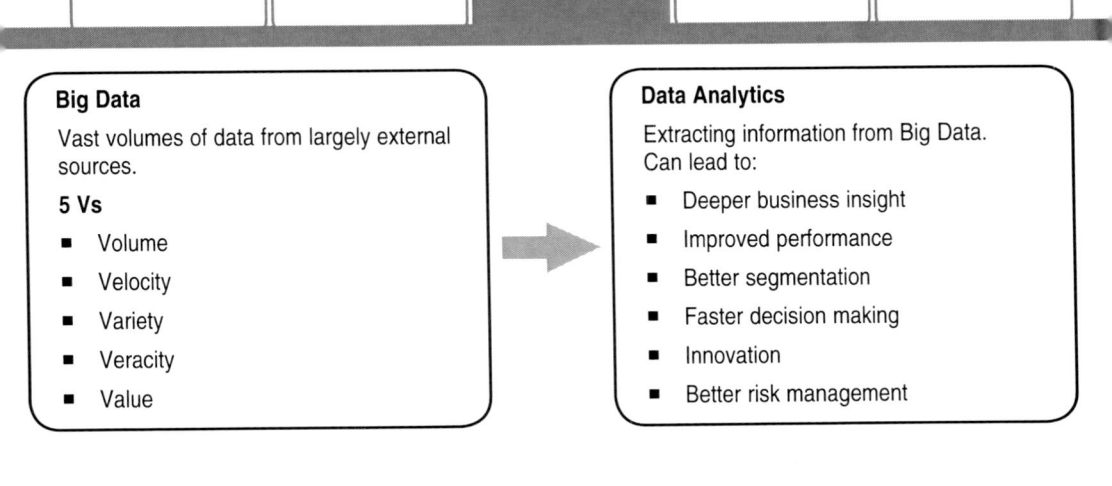

Big Data

Vast volumes of data from largely external sources.

5 Vs

- Volume
- Velocity
- Variety
- Veracity
- Value

Data Analytics

Extracting information from Big Data.
Can lead to:

- Deeper business insight
- Improved performance
- Better segmentation
- Faster decision making
- Innovation
- Better risk management

Data protection principles

1. Lawfulness, fairness, and transparency
2. Purpose limitation
3. Data minimisation
4. Accuracy
5. Storage limitation
6. Integrity and confidentiality
7. Accountability

Processing data

- Data controllers – process data
- Data processors – process on behalf of data controllers
- Data subjects – identifiable individuals whose data is being processed
- Non-compliance can lead to:
  - Criminal conviction
  - Fines up to £18m, or 4% of global turnover

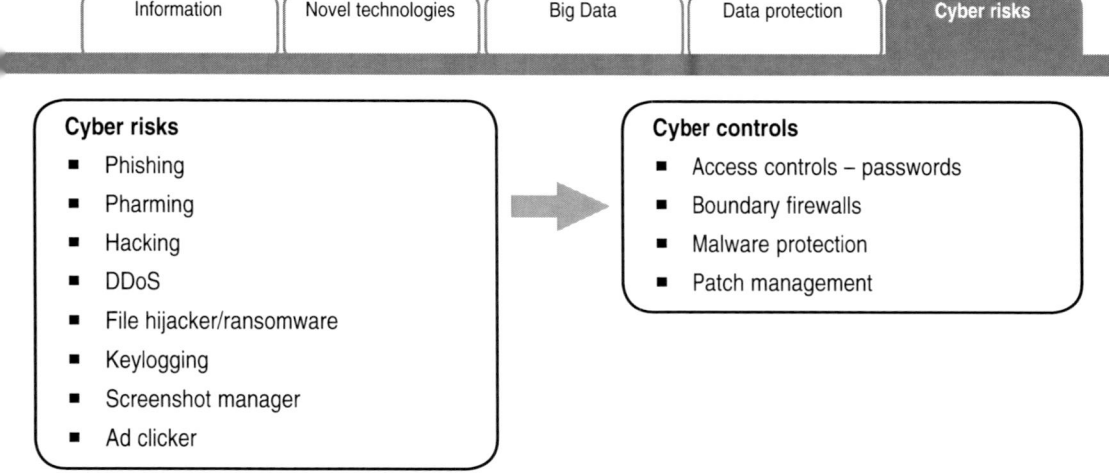

Cyber risks

- Phishing
- Pharming
- Hacking
- DDoS
- File hijacker/ransomware
- Keylogging
- Screenshot manager
- Ad clicker

Cyber controls

- Access controls – passwords
- Boundary firewalls
- Malware protection
- Patch management

7: Communicating data

Exam questions may focus on:

1 *Explaining the importance of professional skills in business communications.*

2 *Identify the most appropriate form of communication in a given scenario.*

3 *Describe the various data visualisation tools available.*

4 *Identify the most appropriate data visualisation tools to use in a given scenario.*

5 *Interpret a data set you have been supplied with, identifying trends and patterns within.*

Communication process

- Sender to recipient
- Horizontal
- Vertical
- Diagonal

Appropriateness

- Format
- House styles
- Professional presentation
- Technically correct
- Understandable
- Corporate image
- Achieves its purpose

Professional communication

- Meet stakeholder requirements
- Appropriate for desired outcome
- Communicate valid information
- Importance of confidentiality

Data visualisation

Presenting data in a visual format

- Increased accessibility
- Real-time data keeps users up to date
- Faster decision making
- Easier to spot patterns

Visualisation tools

- Tables
  - Organising data
- Bar charts
  - Comparing item sizes
- Pie charts
  - Show relative sizes
- Line graphs
  - Relationship between two variables
- Matrices
  - Show relationship between items

Notes

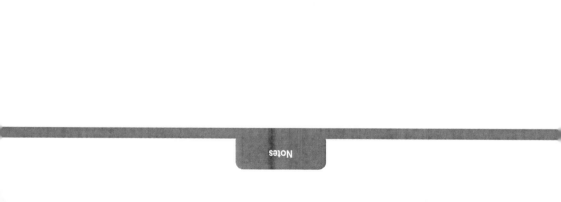

Notes

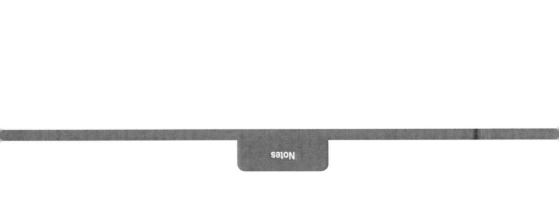

Notes

Notes